Baseball by the Numbers

By Richie Chevat

CELEBRATION PRESS
Pearson Learning Group

Contents

Stats and Bats

Have you ever been to a baseball game? Do you know someone who is a baseball fan? If so, chances are you noticed something about the game of baseball—it's full of numbers.

No other sport uses numbers more than baseball. Just about everything that can be counted in a baseball game is counted. Every time a player gets a hit, it goes in the record books. Every time a batter strikes out, it's recorded. Every time a **fielder** misses a catch, it gets written down. All of these numbers are baseball **statistics**.

Fans who follow a team closely might know each player's statistics.

Joe DiMaggio

Card Statistics

Baseball cards are popular with fans and collectors. Each card gives statistics for a featured player. Here are meanings for some abbreviations:

W	wins
L	losses
ERA	earned run average
AVG	batting average
HR	home runs
GS	games started
CG	complete games
SHO	shutouts
SV	saves
IP	innings pitched
H	hits
BB	walks (bases on balls)
SO	strikeouts
S	singles
E	errors

Some baseball numbers have become famous. Say the number 56 to baseball fans, and they will reply, "Joe DiMaggio." That's because in 1941, Joe DiMaggio got a hit in every game for fifty-six straight games. That hitting streak is a record that still stands today.

This book will help you understand some of the most common baseball statistics, or stats. You'll learn how baseball statistics got started and how they are used today. You'll meet some of the great athletes who created those stats. You'll see why baseball is a game of numbers.

From Town Ball to Baseball

Baseball began more than 200 years ago in Colonial America. European settlers brought over games they played with a stick and a ball. The games had names like **cricket**, rounders, and town ball.

In 1845, a group of players in New York City began to write down the rules of a game they called baseball. Almost immediately, newspapers began reporting baseball games and statistics. The first game resembling modern baseball took place on June 19, 1846. The score was New York Nine 23, New York Knickerbockers 1. The game they played looked like baseball, but the rules were different.

a baseball game in the 1800s

5

In 1856, a young reporter named Henry Chadwick saw a baseball game in Hoboken, New Jersey. Chadwick began to report on baseball for his newspaper. He began to find new ways of recording and **comparing** what the players did on the field.

One of his lasting inventions was the box score. The box score is a chart that reporters or fans use to record what happens in a baseball game. It lets you see at a glance how individuals and a team performed. Henry Chadwick's box score is still used today almost unchanged, 150 years later.

Henry Chadwick, inventor of the box score, is sometimes called the "Father of Baseball."

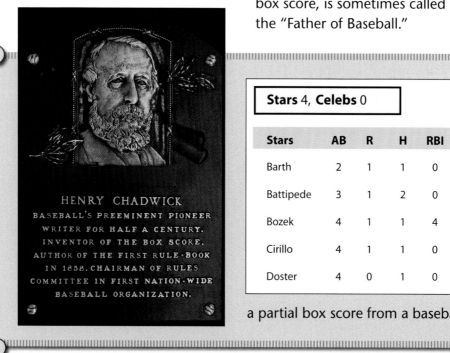

HENRY CHADWICK
BASEBALL'S PREEMINENT PIONEER
WRITER FOR HALF A CENTURY.
INVENTOR OF THE BOX SCORE.
AUTHOR OF THE FIRST RULE-BOOK
IN 1858. CHAIRMAN OF RULES
COMMITTEE IN FIRST NATION-WIDE
BASEBALL ORGANIZATION.

Stars 4, Celebs 0							

Stars	AB	R	H	RBI	BB	SO	Avg
Barth	2	1	1	0	1	1	.330
Battipede	3	1	2	0	1	0	.282
Bozek	4	1	1	4	0	0	.284
Cirillo	4	1	1	0	0	1	.297
Doster	4	0	1	0	0	0	.290

a partial box score from a baseball game

By 1895, baseball guides were published so a growing number of baseball fans could compare stats.

In early baseball, fielding was a lot more important than pitching. Fielders did not wear gloves, so catching the ball was a lot harder.

Reporters like Chadwick kept track of four different ways fielders got runners out: 1) balls caught on the fly; 2) balls caught on a bounce; 3) runners **tagged** out at base; 4) runners tagged out while running. There were no stats for pitchers at all.

By 1863, reporters were counting the number of times fielders missed a play. They called these *Catches Missed*. Later, they were called *Errors of Fielding*. Today, they are simply known as errors.

Henry Chadwick tried to design statistics that let fans compare players on different teams. However, it was another sportswriter named H. A. Dobson who invented a new way to compare players. In 1872, Dobson invented the batting **average**. You figure a player's batting average by dividing the number of hits by the number of times at bat. A player who had 210 hits and 560 at-bats would have a batting average of .375.

(570)	Bees	Redbirds	Knights	Cobras	Suns	Season Totals	Career Totals
G	11	12	7	11	9	50	100
AB	36	47	27	41	31	182	364
R	3	5	3	4	3	18	36
H	10	12	7	9	6	44	88
2B	2	2	0	0	1	5	10
3B	0	1	0	0	0	1	2
HR	1	0	0	1	0	2	4
RBI	8	13	2	3	1	27	54
SB	0	0	1	1	0	2	4
SLG	.417	.340	.259	.293	.226	.307	.307
BB	3	3	2	3	3	14	28
SO	2	5	2	4	5	18	36
AVG	.278	.255	.229	.220	.194	.235	.235

Third Base • Pearson Celebs
Roberto Dobarero
5'9" 185 lbs Bats: Right Throws: Right
Draft: Cardinals #7   June 2005
Acq: Free Agent Born: Los Angeles July 16, 1982

A typical baseball card showing statistics for a player's season and career totals. An actual Major League card would show more games played in a season.

Figuring a Batting Average

Look at the example of a player who had 210 hits and 560 at-bats:

210 hits ÷ 560 at-bats = .375 batting average

Hits only include the times a batter gets on base by hitting safely without an error by the defense. So, for example, it does not include walks. It also does not include times a batter is out but advances runners. That happens with a sacrifice fly—when a runner scores even though the ball is caught in the outfield.

The Cheat Who Changed Baseball

Pitchers were not important in the first baseball games. They were supposed to softly **lob** the ball toward the batter. Batters could ask for a high pitch or a low pitch. A young player named Jim Creighton changed the role of pitchers forever. He did it by cheating.

Creighton was eighteen when he started pitching for the Brooklyn Excelsiors. Instead of gently tossing the ball toward home plate, Creighton snapped his wrist at the last second. He did it so quickly it was hard for the **umpires** to spot it. Creighton began getting batters out by whizzing the ball past them. Fans loved it. Sports writers and fans had something new to count: strikeouts.

Thanks to Jim Creighton, baseball is very different for pitchers such as the Orioles' Bruce Chen, shown here.

Other pitchers copied Creighton's pitching style. Another Excelsior player, Candy Cummings, invented the curve ball in 1867. By 1884, pitchers were allowed to throw overhand.

Players had to learn to hit the new pitches, and batting averages became very important. Players weren't considered really good unless they hit an average of .300 or above. Some people, including Henry Chadwick, worried that players were thinking only about their own records and not about winning games for their teams.

Batting averages went up and down depending on rule changes. In 1881, the pitcher was moved farther from home plate—from 45 feet to 50 feet. Batting averages went up.

What's in a Curve Ball?

Many pitchers can throw a ball that changes direction as it travels. They can do this by snapping their wrist and fingers slightly as they throw the ball. This makes the ball spin, which causes the ball to curve. The direction of the ball depends on the direction and speed of the spin. The batter who doesn't see this curve has a hard time hitting the ball with any force.

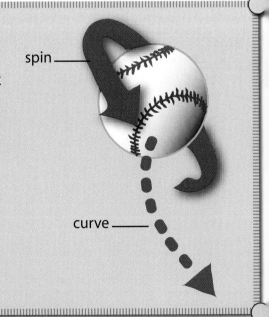

spin

curve

Then along came a pitcher named Cy Young who threw so hard that he left batters and umpires staring. Thanks to Young and other powerful pitchers, batting averages went down again. In 1893, the pitcher's mound was placed where it is today: 60 feet 6 inches from home plate. As a result, in 1894 the entire National League averaged over .300.

Cy Young won 511 games, the most in major league history.

ERA (Earned Run Average)

One of the ways a pitcher is measured is by his earned run average. This statistic compares the number of runs a pitcher allowed with the number of innings he pitched. (An earned run is a run that scores without an error by a fielder.) To find a pitcher's earned run average, multiply the number of earned runs he has allowed by 9. Then, divide that number by the number of innings pitched. Finally, round the number to the second decimal place. Pitchers want a low ERA. In 1997, Roger Clemens allowed 60 earned runs and pitched in 264 innings.

$$60 \times 9 = 540$$
$$540 \div 264 = 2.05$$

His earned run average for the season was 2.05—the best in the American League that year.

Anything but Average Players

By 1900, the rules of baseball were pretty much what they are today. It was also a time when some of baseball's biggest numbers were put in the record books.

These records were set by players like Ty Cobb. Cobb started his career with the Detroit Tigers in 1905. His lifetime batting average of .367 is still the highest ever.

In 1910, it was announced that the major league hitter with the highest batting average would win a new car. With two games left to play in the season, Ty Cobb felt the car was his. He decided to sit out the last two games.

Ty Cobb

Cobb's **rival** was Napoleon Lajoie of Cleveland. In Cleveland's last two games, the manager of the opposing team told his third baseman to play very deep. This allowed Lajoie to **bunt** and get on base seven times. Had he beaten his rival's batting average?

The season was over, but no one knew who had won the batting contest. It took days to find out that Lajoie had batted .384, but Cobb had batted .385. Because of the controversy created by the contest, each player was given a new car.

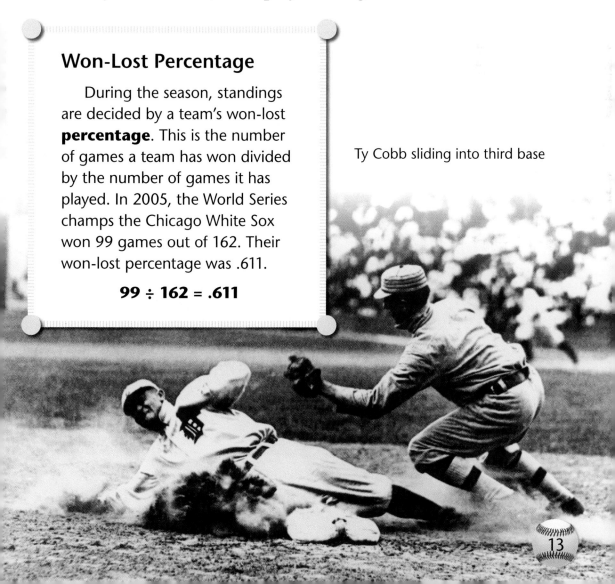

Won-Lost Percentage

During the season, standings are decided by a team's won-lost **percentage**. This is the number of games a team has won divided by the number of games it has played. In 2005, the World Series champs the Chicago White Sox won 99 games out of 162. Their won-lost percentage was .611.

$$99 \div 162 = .611$$

Ty Cobb sliding into third base

A **decade** later, batting averages had sunk once again. Pitchers used all sorts of tricks like scratching the ball or spitting on it. Those tricks made the ball move in strange ways. Home runs were so unusual that no one kept count of them.

Then, in 1915, a player for the Boston Red Sox began hitting home runs. His name was Babe Ruth. Ruth smashed the ball as no one else had done before.

Sports writers believed the season record for home runs was 25. Ruth broke that record in 1919. Then someone discovered that a player had hit 27 home runs in 1884. So Ruth had to break the record for the second time that season. He did and finished with 29.

Babe Ruth, also called "The Sultan of Swat," hit balls out of the park—something rarely done at that time.

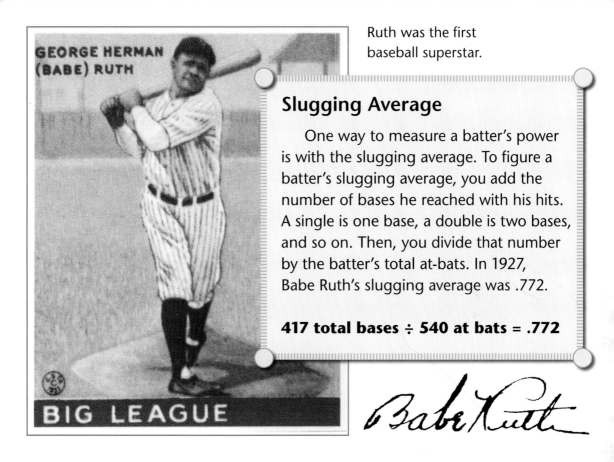

GEORGE HERMAN (BABE) RUTH

BIG LEAGUE

Ruth was the first baseball superstar.

Slugging Average

One way to measure a batter's power is with the slugging average. To figure a batter's slugging average, you add the number of bases he reached with his hits. A single is one base, a double is two bases, and so on. Then, you divide that number by the batter's total at-bats. In 1927, Babe Ruth's slugging average was .772.

417 total bases ÷ 540 at bats = .772

Babe Ruth

The fans loved the excitement of the homer. The club owners changed the ball to make it easier for players to hit it farther. They used a new kind of wool that could be wound tighter inside the ball. The new "lively" ball traveled farther when it was hit. The owners also outlawed scratching or spitting on the ball.

Other players copied Ruth's style and began to hit home runs. However, no one hit them like Ruth. In 1920, Ruth, now playing for the New York Yankees, hit 54 homers. In 1921, he hit an amazing 59. In 1927, he hit 60 in one season. That record would last for decades, until 1961.

Pitchers were scared of Ted Williams. He was walked more times than any other player in history, except Babe Ruth.

Babe Ruth was a **slugger** who aimed for the fences. Ted Williams was a hitter who tried to make batting a science. Williams hit a lot of home runs (521), but he is best known for getting a lot of hits.

Williams was known for his incredible eyesight. He was also known for practicing and working hard. His work paid off with a lifetime batting average of .344. That's number six on the all-time list.

In 1941, Ted Williams, who played for the Red Sox, was working on another record. He became the last player to hit over .400 in one season.

On the last day of the 1941 season, Williams's batting average was .39955. There was a **doubleheader** that day, and his manager offered to let Williams sit it out. That way the League would round his average up to .400.

Williams insisted on playing. "If I can't really do it, I don't want it," he said. He played in both games, got 6 hits, and finished with a season average of .406.

RBI (Runs Batted In)

In Ted Williams's rookie year, he hit 145 RBIs. RBI stands for runs batted in. It counts how many runs a player drives in. It's one way of measuring how much a player is helping the team to score runs.

Ted Williams thought that batting was a science that could be studied and taught.

Baseball: Science or Art?

From the days of Henry Chadwick, baseball writers and fans had studied statistics. The only people who did not seem to study them were baseball managers.

Managers have to make lots of decisions during a game. They set the batting order, or lineup. They decide how deep the fielders will play and when a batter will bunt. For years, they made all these decisions based on their "gut."

In 1968, Earl Weaver, manager of the Baltimore Orioles, began to keep records. Then he used those statistics to decide who would be in the game.

Earl Weaver was one of the first managers to keep statistics on all of his batters.

Weaver kept his records on paper index cards. He stored the cards in a plastic box and brought them into the dugout with him. Some managers made fun of Weaver and his cards. They said that baseball was an art. They said they weren't going to make decisions based on numbers. However, other managers thought that Weaver was on to something. They began using computers instead of index cards.

One team, the Oakland A's, decided to take things even further. Managers shouldn't rely on guesses or hunches, they said. Instead, cold, hard numbers would tell them what to do.

The Oakland A's based their lineups on stats.

On-Base Percentage

Some managers believe that a batting average is not the best way to judge a player. They think a better stat to use is on-base percentage. Unlike batting average, on-base percentage counts not only regular hits, but also walks and hits by pitcher. (If a player is hit by a pitch, he goes to first base.) You figure on-base percentage by adding hits, walks, and hits by pitcher. You then add his at-bats, walks, hits by pitch, and sacrifice flies. Divide the first number (hits + walks + hits by pitcher) by the second number (at-bats + walks + hits by pitcher + sacrifice flies).

As an example, in 2005, Derek Jeter's batting average was .309, but his on-base percentage was .389.

This new method of managing baseball says you don't win ball games with big plays. You don't gamble by stealing a base or hitting a sacrifice fly. You play each game the same way, by looking at the numbers. You may lose a game or two, but in the long run, you will win.

While parts of this new method have caught on, only a couple of teams have really used it. Most managers believe that baseball will never be a game of just numbers. There will always be decisions that just come from the gut.

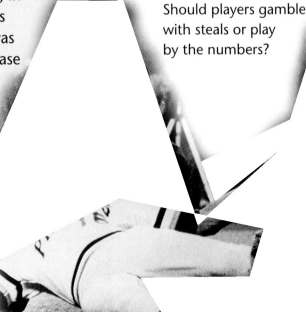

Should players gamble with steals or play by the numbers?

Fantasy Baseball

These days, thanks to statistics, computers, and the Internet, anyone can be a manager of a major league baseball team. Not a real team, of course, but a fantasy team. Millions of people play in fantasy baseball leagues.

You create your team by picking real-life baseball players from the major league teams. You can pick any player from any team.

The success of your team depends on how the real-life players do in real games. You add the stats for your players to see how well your fantasy team is doing. In fantasy baseball, stats are more important than anything else. It doesn't matter if real-life teams win or lose. All that matters is your players' stats.

In fantasy baseball, teams are made up of real players from the major leagues.

· Customize · Sign Out · Help   ● Web ● SportsLine ○ Player [   ] [SEARCH]

Fantasy Baseball

Home | NFL | NBA | MLB | NHL | Coll FB | Coll BK | PGA TOUR | Autos | Tennis | Horses | More + | **Fantasy** | SPiN | Games | Contests | Shop

League Home | Scoreboard | Standings | Stats | Teams | Players | Transactions | Injuries | Options | Help

Sortable Stats

Sortable Stats · League Leaders · Last Six · Versus   Save Print Sheet Send

Players: [Big Red Machine] Timeframe: [Year to Date] Data Source: [Fantasy] Stats: [Standard]

BIG RED MACHINE PLAYERS YEAR TO DATE FANTASY STANDARD STATS

Player	AB	R	H	HR	RBI	BB	SB	BA	OBP	SLG
Barfield, Josh 2B SD	8	1	3	0	0	0	0	0.3750	0.3750	0.3750
Blalock, Hank 3B TEX	14	2	5	1	3	2	0	0.3571	0.4375	0.5714
Floyd, Cliff LF NYM	12	2	3	0	1	2	1	0.2500	0.3571	0.3333
Howard, Ryan 1B PHI	11	2	3	1	1	2	0	0.2727	0.3846	0.5455
Ibanez, Raul LF SEA	15	3	6	0	2	3	0	0.4000	0.5000	0.6000
Lee, Carlos N. LF MIL	9	3	4	1	2	4	0	0.4444	0.6154	0.8889
Lopez, Felipe SS CIN	12	1	4	0	1	3	0	0.3333	0.4667	0.4167
Mauer, Joe C MIN	8	3	3	0	0	1	1	0.3750	0.4444	0.3750
Monroe, Craig RF DET	12	1	2	1	2	0	0	0.1667	0.2308	0.4167
Pujols, Albert 1B STL	10	5	5	3	6	4	1	0.5000	0.6000	1.4000
Reyes, Jose B. SS NYM	14	3	4	0	2	1	1	0.2857	0.3333	0.4286
Rowand, Aaron OF PHI	10	1	2	0	0	1	0	0.2000	0.2727	0.3000
Wilkerson, Brad B. OF TEX	19	4	4	1	1	0	1	0.2105	0.2105	0.4211

The Greatest Ever?

Can we use statistics to see who is the greatest player of all time? So many things have changed since 1845. Statistics don't always tell the whole story.

One of the most famous records in baseball was Babe Ruth's single-season record of 60 home runs. For more than 30 years, that record went untouched. Then, a New York Yankees slugger named Roger Maris hit 61 home runs in 1961.

However, many fans said Ruth's record wasn't broken. Why? The baseball season was longer in 1961

than in 1927. Maris had eight extra games to hit those 61 homers.

Statistics can't prove everything. Still, they're part of the fun of baseball.

Roger Maris

Glossary

average the number found by adding all the numbers in a set and dividing by the number of values

bunt to bat a pitched baseball so lightly that the ball goes only a short distance

cricket a game played with a bat, a ball, and two bases, or wickets

comparing deciding how two people or things are like or unlike each other

decade a period of ten years

doubleheader two games played one after another on the same day

fielder a baseball player in a defensive position on the field

lob a slow, high toss or throw

percentage a fraction in which 100 is the denominator

rival a person who wants and tries to get the same as another; one who tries to equal or do better than another

slugger a baseball player known for hitting home runs

statistics numerical data or facts

tagged in baseball, touched a runner with the ball to make an out

umpires people who rule on the plays in games

Index